Flower Design Made Easy

Also by June Kahl:
A Sketchbook of Easy Flower Designs
A Sketchbook of Creativity in Flower Design

FLOWER DESIGN MADE EASY

June Robison Kahl

Illustrated by Ellen Parsons

Prospect Hill Press
Baltimore, Maryland

1   S

ACKNOWLEDGEMENTS

My sincere thanks to all those friends and family members who gave me their encouragement and support in order to make this book possible, and to Thelma Bauer, florist, for her beautiful flowers.

To those garden club friends who were so generous with their plant material and containers.

To the editor of Prospect Hill Publishing Company and the illustrator for their editorial assistance and artistic decisions.

To the photographer, Eleanor Heldrich, for capturing the spirit of the book.

To the National Council of State Garden Clubs for providing the opportunity for me to become a Master Flower Show Judge.

I wish to thank the National Council of State Garden Clubs, Inc. for permission to use excerpts from certain of their definitions of flower designs.

Copyright 1990 by June Robison Kahl

Printed in the United States of America

ISBN 0-941526-07-0

Library of Congress Catalog Card Number 90-52653

Book design by Ellen Parsons

Published by Prospect Hill Press
216 Wendover Road
Baltimore, Maryland 21218
(301) 889-0320

Table of Contents

DEDICATION

To my grandchildren Stephanie and Erik

Introduction

Learning the basics is the foundation of all flower arranging. A child has to crawl before he walks. So it is with flower designing, which is an art form using plant material. Three different techniques have to be mastered before it is possible to become a confident flower arranger: first, selecting the plant material and coordinating the types of flowers as well as the colors; second, conditioning the plant material; namely, removing broken and damaged leaves and flowers and standing them in water several hours or overnight before arranging in a design; third is the actual making of the designs—over and over again to acquire the ease and confidence to handle fresh and dried plant material.

Once the basics have become automatic, it is time to try the more advanced creative designs which still require the use of the basic elements and principles of flower design. However, now the designer has the creative freedom to express his or her own imagination and originality.

Creative designing comes from within one's own imagination, followed by the desire to express these imaginative thoughts. Developing the ideas and the ability to execute and carry out these ideas in flower design is the aim of this book.

To stimulate the mind, visit a museum sculpture garden or court. Walk around and absorb the beauty of the sculptures. Sketch or photograph six of them. Then plan the design division of a flower show using the six sketches or photographs as inspiration for each of six design classes. Each sculpture's form or shape will suggest a class and the type of plant material to be used. Next, sketch a flower design for one of the classes. This exercise has a twofold purpose. It stimulates the creative mind and it helps train the eye to see the possibilities of using plant material in unusual ways.

Try to associate experiences and impressions with flowers and branches. For example, Queen Anne's lace swaying in the breeze might suggest a ballet. In flower arranging this could be the inspiration for a parallel design.

Work with plant material just for the fun of creating with it. In the middle of the growing season, cut many pieces of the roadside weed mullein, as long as possible. At this time, mullein will be soft and green in color. Later it becomes hard and dark brown. Let the mullein lie outside on the ground in the full sun for several days until it becomes pliable enough to manipulate and be wired into desired shapes. These could be circles, angles, or even initials such as P and S. Think what fun it would be to incorporate initials into flower designs for a party! Let the shaped mullein dry flat on a table or floor. When it is completely dry, spray paint it with flat white paint. After the white paint dries, spray it any color desired. The flat white paint is used as a base coat to seal the natural color of the plant material. By doing this, one achieves a true final color.

Visit as many flower shows as possible and ask for the flower show schedules in order to see how the arrangers used their creative ability to interpret show themes and class titles. Study the size relationships between the designs and their backgrounds; the variation and forms of the plant materials; and the color coordination between the flowers, containers, and backgrounds. Ask yourself if all the elements of design—light, space, line, form, size, color, texture, and pattern—have been organized according to recognized design principles of balance, proportion, scale, rhythm, dominance, and contrast. These are the questions each flower show judge considers while judging a flower design.

The designs in this book need not be duplicated exactly. Be selective. Choose those ideas from the book that can be adapted to your own containers and for placement in your own home. Keep a sketchbook of the designs that you create as well as the material used. It will become a good source of information for your later use.

The techniques for making flower show backgrounds explained in the book make it easy for a designer to create backgrounds using a few simple tools such as a matknife, double stick tape, construction paper, etc.

There are many designs to be studied and created. Any art object in your possession can become a feature in a flower design. Just remember that the object must dominate the plant material.

The National Council of State Garden Clubs in its latest HANDBOOK FOR FLOWER SHOWS has included some new creative designs. The handbook states, "Traditional designs are an art form *in* space while Creative designs are an art form *of* space with solids and spaces becoming one." Included in this book are four of these new designs; namely, creative line, transparency, eclectic, and parallel. The definition of each of these new designs will be at the beginning of the text for that particular design.

The new creative designs allow more freedom of expression. A creative line design uses a minimum of plant material and sometimes emphasizes the beauty of an individual bloom or foliage. An interesting option for the designer is the use of man-made or found objects for line material. A parallel design requires at least three or more vertical groupings of materials. Units may be composed of one plant material, a combination of materials, or the same plant material in each unit. These two types of designs are beautiful when adapted for use on a dining room table.

A good choice for a large design is the eclectic design. This design combines two different designs into a new concept. For example, a vertical and a mass combination or a vertical and a horizontal.

Use all of the designs in this book as stimuli for your own creative designing.

Flower Arranger's Workbasket

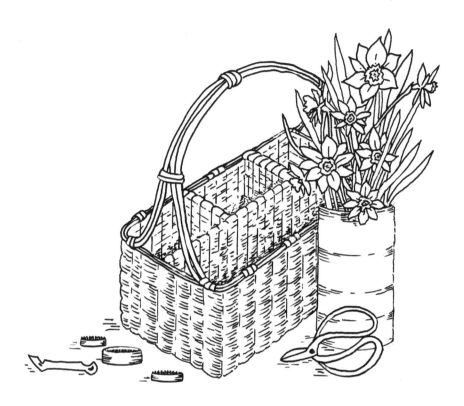

A flower arranger is an artist working with live plant material; and, like any artist, he or she will need some basic tools and equipment. Keeping everything together in one place, ready to use, is the function of an arranger's workbasket. It should include:

1. Flower scissors with sharp, straight blades to cut stems so they can absorb water easily.

2. Pinholders and pincups—to hold flowers.

3. Floral clay—to attach pinholders to containers.

4. Floral foam—to hold flowers in containers when pinholders cannot be used.

5. Can opener—to remove pinholders from containers.

6. Floral wire (straight) of medium gauge (#20)—to hold plant material in place.

7. Tall container—for water to condition flowers.

To Prepare Plant Material

1. Flowers should be fresh and at the height of their perfection.
2. Condition all flowers immediately by cutting off at least one inch of stem, preferably under water. Strip off bottom leaves and place in a deep container of tepid water. Leave in water several hours or overnight to harden before arranging.
    Exception: daffodils require shallow water.
3. Wash all foliage to remove dust. Remove broken or damaged leaves.
4. Start with a clean container and pinholder.
5. Sit with container directly in front of you.
6. Attach pinholder to dry container.
7. Fill container with water before you start to make a design.
8. Remember that the first placement is the most important. Select the most beautiful and the strongest of the plant material marked in each design for #1.
9. Supplies may be purchased from florist or garden center.

To Attach a Pinholder

1. To attach a pinholder to a dry container, first roll a piece of floral clay, between both hands, into a long, slender cigarette shape.
2. Attach this roll of clay to the outer edge of an upside down pinholder, making sure you join the two ends of clay together.
3. Place the pinholder in the container and press down hard, giving it a slight twist. This will create suction, which holds the pinholder in place.

To Bend Fresh Plant Material

1. Start halfway up stem.
2. Place both thumbs touching underneath stem with other fingers over top of stem.
3. Gently apply pressure.
4. Keep applying pressure while moving fingers up to end of the branch.
5. Repeat this procedure until the stem is bent as much as desired.
6. To make a loop, bring tip around until it crosses main stem. Cut a 1½" piece of medium-gauge florist wire. Bend the piece of wire around the main stem and the tip of the plant material. The turns of the wire should be as neat and close together as possible. Do not twist wire—simply bend it around the stems.

To Dry Plant Material

DRYING IN WATER

This method may be used for plants with exceptionally strong stems such as yarrow, hydrangea, and many grasses. Pick the flowers just before they begin to dry on the plant—at the height of their beauty. Keep them in a container of water until they dry.

GLYCERINE

Mix one part glycerine to two parts hot water. Crush or split the ends of branches and immerse them in 3" or 4" of the solution until the leaves change color. This is the best method for preserving leaves such as beech or aspidistra.

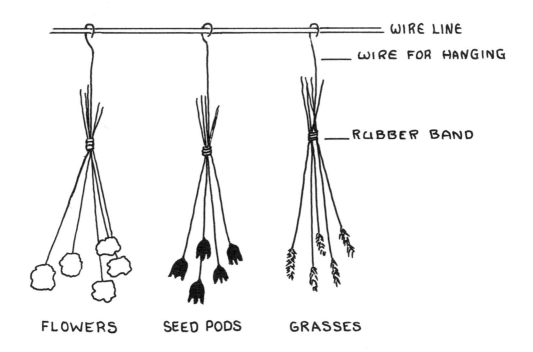

FLOWERS   SEED PODS   GRASSES

AIR DRYING

Strip the leaves from the stems of flowers. Bind them together with rubber bands, and hang by bunches upside down in a cool, dry, dark place. Easy plant material to dry—hardy annuals, grasses, seed pods. Make sure that air is able to circulate around the flower heads. Wire each bunch to a plastic-coated wire clothesline.

BORAX AND SAND

Mix two parts Borax to one part sand in a container with a cover. Cut off all but 1″ of the stems. Place flower heads upside down in the Borax and sand, making sure the mixture is worked in and around all the flower petals. Keep the top on the box while drying flowers.

SILICA GEL

The method is the same as for Borax and sand. This is the most expensive method; however, it is also the most popular because silica gel acts quickly—within 48 to 72 hours. There are several brands available.

To Wire Grapes

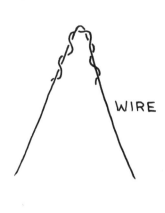 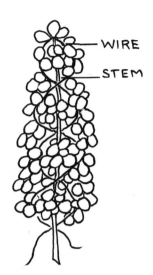

When grapes are wired they acquire grace and support so they can be attached securely to other parts of a design.

1. Connect two pieces of straight floral wire to form a V shape.
2. Place the wire on the table with the open end of the V facing toward you.
3. Pick up a cluster of grapes by the stem and place them on top of the wire with two or three grapes at the bottom of the cluster extending over the pointed end of the V.
4. Take one end of the wire in each hand. Bring the wire up through the grapes to the top, crossing over the grapes.
5. Change hands on the wire and go down through the grapes, crossing over again.
   NOTE: The process is similar to lacing a shoe.
6. Continue in this manner until the grapes are wired to the top of the stem.
7. After reaching the top, take both wires in one hand and twist them around the stem.
8. Some designs may require a longer wire for fixing the grapes into place, so a third wire may be added to the two wires that are twisted around the stem of the grapes.

Section I

The Basics

Flower arranging is an art form using fresh, dried and/or treated plant material. Basic flower design teaches how to select plant material, the care and condtioning of flowers, as well as how to make the basic styles such as mass, vertical, in the Oriental manner; and, finally, creative.

In traditional American designs the larger flowers are placed at the bottom while the smaller ones are placed at the top and outer edges. Color is used in the same way—the darker colors are placed at the bottom while the lighter colors are placed at the outer edges.

In a vertical deisgn, the plant material has an upward thrust that is exaggerated so that it has greater height than width.

Each country has its own characteristics in flower design. The English mass is rounded and loosely arranged. The French mass is usually oval in shape, larger at the bottom and smaller at the top. The word abundant best describes the Dutch mass, which is large with a massing of all flower forms of rich colors and the use of many varied accessories.

Oriental designs are typically asymmetrical with a minimum of plant material and emphasis on line.

Creative designs are the result of a creative idea of the arranger. These designs usually show restraint in the amount of plant material and other components used. The arranger is given complete freedom and is not bound by rules, styles, or traditional patterns.

By mastering the basics, one acquires a certain ease and joy in creating flower designs.

Design 1

Mass designs are characterized by the use of a large quantity of plant material. The plant material is not crowded but the design has a closed silhouette.

SUPPLIES

Round container, 10″ diameter

Pinholder, 4″ diameter

Floral clay

PLANT MATERIAL

6 yellow gladioli

5 orange carnations with ruffled edges

5 orange spray carnations

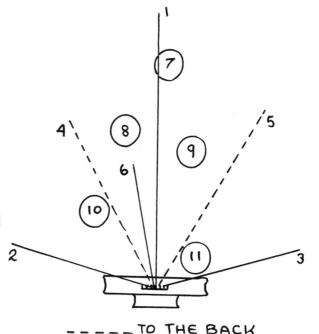

TO THE BACK

PREPARATION

Use floral clay to attach the pinholder to the center of the container. Remove several small buds from the top of each gladiolus. The flower stalks should be straight.

PROCEDURE

Begin with the gladioli, the spike flowers, and place them in a fan pattern with some leaning toward the back and some coming to the front. The gladioli should form a triangle.

Gladiolus #1 is the tallest and is placed in the center back of the pinholder.

Cut #2 gladiolus two thirds the height of #1 and place it low and to the left of #1.

Cut #3 gladiolus the same as #2 and place it low and to the right of #1.

Cut #4 gladiolus shorter than #1 and place it to the left of #1, leaning to the back.

#5 gladiolus is cut shorter than #4 and placed to the right of #1, leaning to the back.

#6 gladiolus is cut shorter than #5 and is placed to the left between #1 and #4, leaning to the front.

Cut #7, large carnation, shorter than #1 and place it to the right back of #1.

#8 carnation is cut shorter than #5 and is placed to the left front of #1.

#9 carnation is cut shorter than #6 and placed to the right of #1 and in front of #5.

#10 carnation is cut shorter than #9 and placed to the left front of #4.

#11 carnation is cut shorter than #10 and placed in the center front between #1 and #5.

The small spray carnations are used as filler flowers to fill the spaces in the design. Each spray is cut into two or three pieces of varying lengths and placed wherever needed. Remember to fill in the back of the design with some of the filler plant material so that the design is completed all around.

NOTE: The taller the #1 flower, the more plant material will be needed to fill in the triangular silhouette.

Design 2

A Vertical Design

A vertical design is one with a strong upward thrust and with greater height than width.

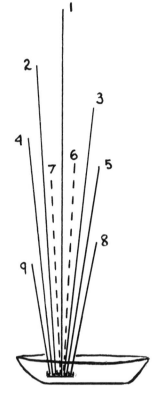

_ _ _ _ TO THE BACK

SUPPLIES

Oval container

Pinholder, 3″ diameter

Floral clay

PLANT MATERIAL

9 purple liatris

3 white alstroemeria sprays

PREPARATION

Attach the pinholder to the container with floral clay. Cut the nine liatris different lengths from 25″ to 8″. For more interest vary the difference in lengths.

Place #1, tallest liatris, in the center of the pinholder.

#2 to the left of #1.

#3 to the right of #1.

#4 to the left of #2.

#5 to the right of #3.

#6 to the back between #1 and #3.

#7 to the back between #1 and #2.

#8 in front of #5.

#9, shortest liatris, to the left front of #4.

Each spray of alstroemeria is cut into individual flowers with stems from 7″ to 4″ in length. Each one is placed individually in several rows around the base of the liatris. Begin with the tallest on the left and work down to the shortest on the right side. Do not overcrowd these flowers.

Design 3

A design in the oriental manner is characterized by restraint in the quantity of plant material used and having an open silhouette. The branches and flowers are arranged gracefully with space between all the components.

SUPPLIES

Low container, 13″ by 9″

Pinholder, 2″ diameter

Floral clay

PLANT MATERIAL

2 white anthurium

3 spirea branches

PREPARATION

Attach pinholder to the upper left corner of the container with floral clay.

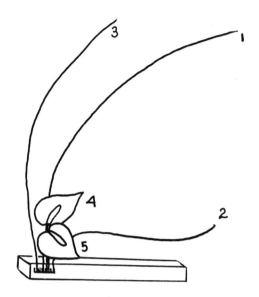

PROCEDURE

Cut branch #1 long enough so that the tip reaches over the right side of the container. Place on the left back of the pinholder.

Cut branch #2 shorter than #1 and place it diagonally opposite #1 and low on the pinholder. The tip should reach over the right front edge of the container.

Cut branch #3 shorter than #2 and place it to the left of #1, going in the same direction as #1.

Cut flower #4 about 7″ long and place in the center of the pinholder leaning forward.

Cut #5 about 5″ long and place in front of #4 leaning forward.

Design 4

A creative design results from a creative idea of the artist, using plant material and other components to organize the design elements within the limits of the principles of good design.

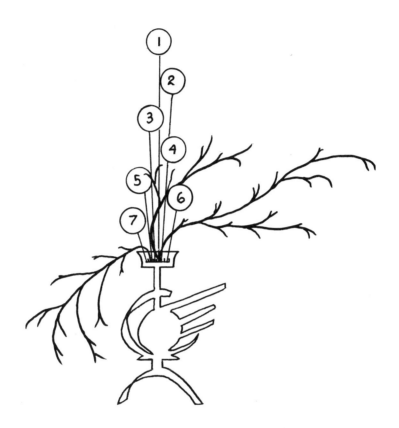

SUPPLIES

Black iron candlestick used for
  container
Black pincup, 3″ diameter
Flat black spray paint
Floral clay

PLANT MATERIAL

7 red carnations
2 citrus trifoliata branches

PREPARATION

Cut one graceful 20″ branch and one short branch of citrus trifoliata. Trim off some of the short side branches to create larger spaces on the branch stem. Spray the branches flat black. Attach the pincup to the top of the candlestick with floral clay.

PROCEDURE

Insert the large branch, leaning horizontally, on the right side of the pincup. The short branch is about one third the length of the large one. Place it, hanging low, on the left in the pincup.

Lay the seven carnations on a table with their stems extending over the table's edge. Arrange them in descending order, each about 2" to 3" shorter than the one before, with #1 about 16" to #7 about 4". Trim the stems even with the edge of the table.

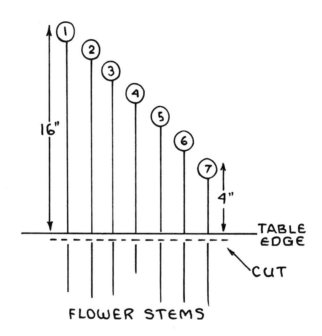

Place #1 upright in the center of the pincup.

    #2 to the right and slightly in front of #1.

    #3 to the left and slightly in front of #1.

    #4 to the right in front of #2.

    #5 to the left in front of #3.

    #6 to the right in front of #4.

    #7 to the left in front of #5.

NOTE: This design could be considered an eclectic design. This means combining two different design styles in one. This combines a vertical design with a horizontal.

Section II

Designs For The Collector

One of the joys of traveling is the opportunity to collect artifacts from the places you are visiting. Each country is known for some particular thing, whether it be crystal, wood, porcelain, or metal. Candlesticks, tableware, art objects, silver or brass pieces are but a few choices. Before leaving for any trip, read about the place, the people, and the products. This way, even before leaving home, you will have a good idea about what would be fun to collect. The flower arranger always thinks about what can be used as a container. Later, every time you use an item from a trip, it is a reminder of the vacation and the place from which the object came.

A collection of candlesticks can develop into a hobby, but when a collection is put to use instead of being packed away in boxes, it becomes an outstanding acquisition.

Candlesticks are fun to collect because they come in many different colors, shapes, and forms. However, they become more interesting when you are able to use them in different ways. For example, try placing them at different locations on the table.

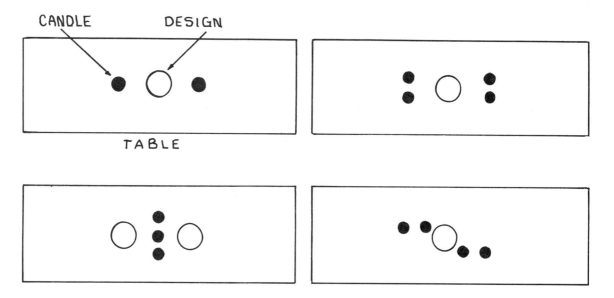

Experiment with using candlesticks as flower containers. Many different types of water-holding adaptors for use in candle holders can be purchased in garden centers and florist shops. Some candlesticks may even be turned upside down with a pincup placed on top to hold the flowers. Candlesticks used as containers can be placed anywhere in the home.

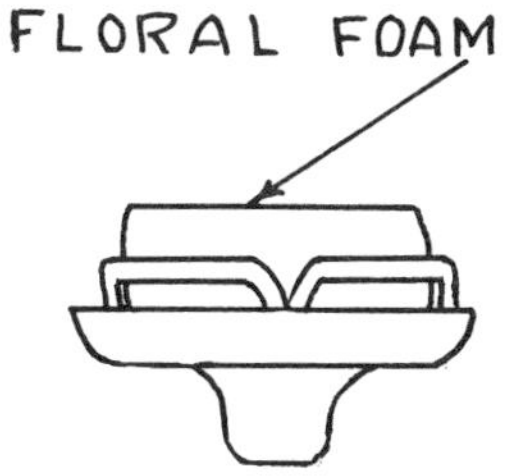

FLORAL FOAM

PLASTIC ADAPTOR

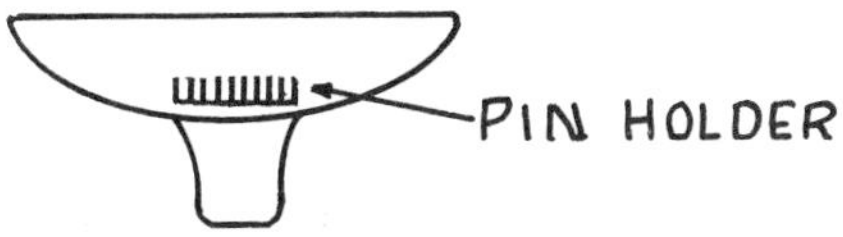

PIN HOLDER

CRYSTAL ADAPTOR

Design 5

A feature is a dominant object in a design other than plant material, container, base, mechanics, background, and/or underlay.

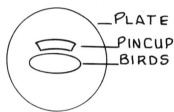

SUPPLIES

Frosted crystal Lalique birds
Blue crystal Stueben plate
Small pinholder

PLANT MATERIAL

3 white dogwood branches
3 white azalea sprigs

PREPARATION

Place the crystal birds in the center of the blue plate and place the pinholder directly in back of the birds. The plate is deep enough to hold water. If it were not, a pincup could be used.

PROCEDURE

Cut the dogwood branches 15″, 12″, and 9″.

Cut the azalea sprigs 7″, 6″, and 5″.

Place #1, 15″ dogwood branch, so it stands high and to the left behind the birds.

Place #2, 9″ dogwood branch, low and to the right of the birds.

Place #3, 12″ dogwood branch, low and to the left of the birds.

The three azalea sprigs are placed low and in between the dogwood branches.

Design 6

Brass Candlesticks From China

SUPPLIES

    2 candlesticks that separate into
        sections

    2 pincups, 2″ diameter

    Floral clay

PLANT MATERIAL

    8 pink carnations

    8 sprengeri stems of various
        lengths

PREPARATION

Condition the sprengeri by immersing it in water overnight.
Separate the parts of the two candlesticks and reassemble them to
make one very tall candlestick and one as short as possible. Place one
pincup in the top of the tall candlestick and one in the top of the short
candlestick. Floral clay may be used if necessary to attach the pincups
to the candlesticks.

PROCEDURE

DESIGN 1

In the pincup on top of the tall candlestick, arrange seven pieces of
sprengeri of various lengths completely around the pincup. (The eighth
piece will be used in Design 2.) Some of the pieces of sprengeri should
reach from the top of the candlestick to within a few inches of the table
surface.

Arrange five carnations so they flow toward the front of the pincup.

Flower #1 is 7″ tall and placed very low in the center front of the
pincup, leaning forward.

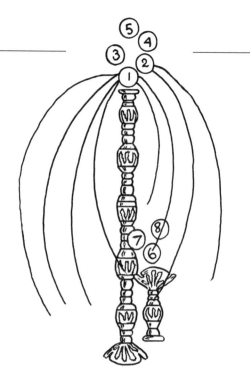

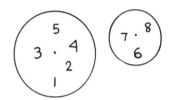

PLACEMENT ON
PINHOLDERS

Flower #2 is 5″ tall and placed slightly higher and to the right of #1.

Flower #3 is 4″ tall and placed slightly higher and to the left of #1.

Flower #4 is 4″ tall and placed slightly higher and to the right of #3.

Flower #5 is 3″ tall and placed almost erect in the center back of the pincup.

DESIGN 2

Arrange three carnations in the pincup on top of the short candlestick so they flow to the front of the pincup.

Flower #6 is 5″ tall and placed very low in the center front of the pincup, leaning forward.

Flower #7 is 4″ tall and placed slightly higher and to the left of #6.

Flower #8 is 3″ tall and placed almost erect in the center back of the pincup.

Cut the last piece of springeri into short pieces and place them in between the flowers.

To assemble the complete design, place the short candlestick very close to the tall candlestick, slightly to the back and underneath the tall design.

VARIATION: The same effect can be obtained by using one tall and one short candlestick.

Design 7

Brass Epergne From India

SUPPLIES

 Epergne
 Round wooden toothpicks
 Wire

PLANT MATERIAL

 Pineapple with a good leaf
  crown
 7 small potatoes
 6 green pears
 12 lady apples
 3 bunches of grapes
 4 lemons

TOOTHPICKS

POTATOES

PREPARATION

The amount of fruit used will vary according to the size of the epergne. The center container and the two side saucers should be lined with plastic to protect them from the fruit. Wire two bunches of grapes according to the directions on page 14. Cut the remaining bunch of grapes into small clusters.

PROCEDURE

CENTER CONTAINER

To make a firm foundation for the fruit, fill the bottom of the container with potatoes. Place one potato in the center and a circle of potatoes around the outside edge.

Insert two toothpicks into each potato in the outer ring. Push the first potato into the center potato, then push the remaining ones into each other.

Insert four toothpicks into the bottom of the pineapple and force the pineapple down on the center potato.

Wire two bunches of grapes to the pineapple by adding long wires to the stems and looping the wires around the pineapple. Arrange the grapes so they hang gracefully over each end of the container. On each side of the pineapple, front and back, place a pear, a lemon, and a second pear in a line so they touch each other. Place the lady apples at random in between the larger fruits. Fill in the remaining spaces with small clusters of grapes. Attach the clusters to the larger fruit with wooden toothpicks.

SIDE SAUCERS

Place a pear, a lemon and a lady apple in each saucer. Fill the empty spaces with small clusters of grapes.

VARIATION: One tall compote and two small bowls could be used for this design.

Design 8

Gold Candlestick From Italy

SUPPLIES

Gold candlestick

Oval green pincup, 5½″ long

Round gold pincup,
   3½″ diameter

PLANT MATERIAL

10 red carnations

6 Japanese holly stems (small leaf)

6 English holly stems (large leaf)

15 white pine sprigs for filler green

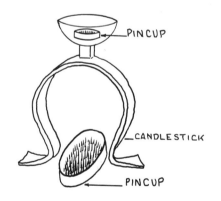

PREPARATION

The candlestick used in this design is 7½″ tall, made of a heavy gold-colored metal. The top is cup-shaped with a diameter of 4½″.

Place the oval pincup directly underneath the candlestick, then place the round pincup on top of the candlestick. Plant material will be both on top and underneath the candlestick.

PROCEDURE

OVAL PINCUP

All of the Japanese holly is placed very low and horizontal, to the right and left of the candlestick.

Cut two #1's of Japanese holly, each 7″ long.

Cut two #2's of Japanese holly, each 5″ long.

Cut two #3's of Japanese holly, each 4″ long.

Bend the bottom inch of each of the six pieces of Japanese holly to a right angle. To keep the holly stems from breaking, wrap the bottom inch and a half of the stem with wire before bending.

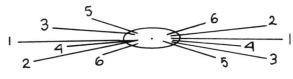

PLACEMENT IN PINCUP

Place one #1 very low in the center on the left side of the oval pincup, pointing outward, and the second #1 very low to the right.

Place the two #2's slightly higher, pointing in the same direction as the #1's, one to the front and one to the back.

Place the two #3's higher, in the same manner as the #2's, one to the back and one to the front.

Cut two #4's of English holly, each 5″ long.

Cut two #5's of English holly, each 4″ long.

Cut two #6's of English holly, each 3″ long.

Working from side to side, insert the the two #4's and the two #5's in the pincup in the same direction as the Japanese holly.

Place the two #6's upright in the center of the pincup. They will be directly underneath the top of the candlestick.

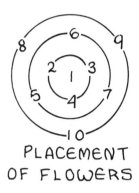

PLACEMENT
OF FLOWERS

ROUND PINCUP

This design is very orderly and precise in the placement of the flowers.

Cut #1 carnation 4″ long and place in the center of the pincup.

Cut #2, #3, and #4 carnations 3½″ long and place in a triangle around #1.

Cut #5, #6, and #7 carnations 3″ long and place in between #2, #3, and #4. Always work toward the outer edge of the pincup.

Cut #8, #9, and #10 carnations 3″ long. Place them low and slightly over the edge of the pincup in the spaces between #5, #6, and #7.

FILLER GREEN

Cut all of the white pine sprigs 3″ long. To give the filler green a neat look, hold each needle tightly in hand and cut off ½″ of the tip.

Place white pine sprigs around each of the flowers, starting in the center and working toward the outer edge. This design should have a very neat and compact look with every space filled with the filler green. The white pine should not be higher than the flowers.

VARIATION: A similar design could be created using one large candlestick with an epergne insert in the center with two oval pincups on each side.

Section III

Backgrounds For A Flower Show

A flower show schedule states whether or not a background is required for a particular class. The background could be made of wood or matboard. It could be covered with paper or fabric. It could be a solid color or patterned. If the schedule says "background to be furnished by the exhibitor," the designer may choose to be creative, using cut-outs and patterned designs, or she may choose a solid color. In either case, the background must complement and not compete with the floral design. A background should never overpower. In a flower show, the flower design is the most important element in the overall picture.

Many times the title of a class will suggest the background. For example, if the title of a class is Blazing Glory, a red matboard could be used. However, it may be more interesting to use a white matboard for the background, with a cut-out design in red mounted on the white. The purpose of the cut-out would be to dramatize the floral design.

Before cutting out a design, always sketch several different possibilities and then decide which would be best for the flower design. The cut-out could be a regular or irregular shape, depending upon the desired effect. For instance:

Class BLAZING GLORY
An irregular cut-out:

Class BLAZING GLORY
A regular cut-out:

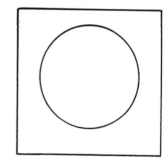

In this section each design is presented as an entry in a design class of a flower show with typical class names and descriptions—as they might be presented in a flower show schedule.

Because the coveted Creativity Award, offered by the National Council of State Garden Clubs for flower shows held under their rules, is given for designs displaying originality and distinction using fresh, dried and/or treated plant material with or without components, each of the illustrated classes would be eligible.

Keep in mind that even though these are designs staged for a flower show, they still have application for special settings in the home such as a hall table, under a favorite picture, on a raised hearth, or in a stairway niche.

Design 9

Class 1   WINDOW TO THE FUTURE
*A creative design using a background to help
interpret the theme.
Eligible for Creativity Award.*

SUPPLIES

Tall creative container

1 brown matboard, 40″ by 32″

1 light yellow matboard, 40″ by
   32″

Matknife

Double stick tape

Wire

PLANT MATERIAL

15 anthuriums

6 Japanese plum yew branches

1 Harry Lauder's Walking Stick

NOTE: The length of the plant material depends upon the height and size of the container which is placed in front of the background. For good design, plant material must stay within the frame of reference; in this case, the background.

PREPARATION OF BACKGROUND

With a matknife, cut out a large circle from the top center section of the brown matboard. Using double stick tape, attach the brown matboard to the yellow matboard.

PROCEDURE

Balance A, the branch of Harry Lauder's Walking Stick, in between

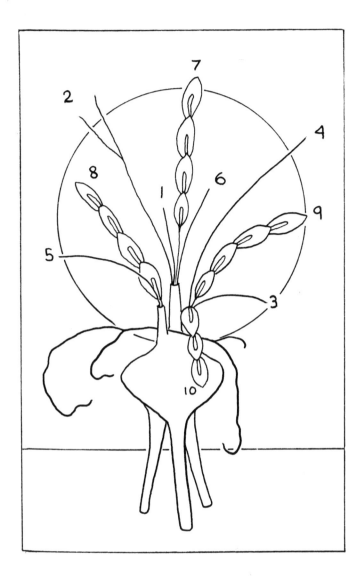

the openings on the top of the container.

Cut yew branches, #1, #2, #3, #4, #5, #6, different lengths and insert them in the openings of the container.

Wire the 15 anthuriums together to form four sprays. Four flowers are used to form #7, #8, and #9. Use three flowers to make #10. Cut flower sprays #7, #8 and #9 different lengths and insert them into the openings of the container. Place spray #10 so it comes forward over the top of the container.

NOTE: More flowers may be used in each spray.

Design 10

Class 2 CIRCLES IN THE SKY
*An elegant design expressing freedom of movement
in both the flower design and the background.
Eligible for Creativity Award.*

SUPPLIES
   Japanese mushroom-shaped
      container
   Pinholder, 3″ diameter
   1 white matboard, 40″ by 32″
   1 medium blue matboard, 40″ by
      32″
   Matknife
   Double stick tape
   Straight pins

PLANT MATERIAL
   5 red ginger flowers
   7 sansevieria leaves

NOTE: The length of plant material depends upon the height and size of
the container which is placed in front of the background. For good
design, plant material must stay within the frame of reference; in this
case, the background.

PREPARATION OF BACKGROUND
   Cut the largest circular shape possible from the white matboard,
making sure it uses the full length of the matboard. Then cut the circle in
half and reverse the halves. Attach the white cut-outs to the blue
background with double stick tape.

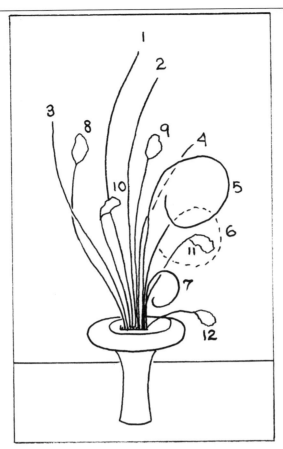

PROCEDURE

Place #1, tallest sansevieria, to the center back on the pinholder.

Cut #2 sansevieria shorter than #1 and place to the right front of #1.

Cut #3 sansevieria shorter than #2 and place to the left front of #1.

Cut #4 sansevieria shorter than #3 and place to the right of #2.

Bend #5 sansevieria into a large circle and secure with a straight pin. Place to the right in front of #4.

Bend #6 sansevieria into a medium circle and secure with a straight pin. Place to the right back of #5.

Bend #7 sansevieria into a small circle and secure with a straight pin. Place in the center in front of #1, leaning forward.

Cut #8 ginger flower shorter than leaf #3 and place to the left of #1.

Cut each succeeding flower shorter than the preceeding one.

Place #9 flower to the right of #2.

Place #10 flower in front of #1.

Place #11 flower so the flower head is in the center of the #6 circle.

Place #12 flower to the right of #7.

41

Design 11

Class 3 HARLEQUIN
*An imaginative design expressing the gaiety and
exaggerated antics of the circus clown.
Background required.
Eligible for Creativity Award.*

SUPPLIES
  Tall candlemold used as a
    container
  Pincup, 4″ diameter
  Floral clay
  1 white matboard, 40″ by 32″
  Matknife
  Black paper
  Double stick tape
  Black spray paint

PLANT MATERIAL
  2 red helaconia flowers
  1 bunch of baby's breath

PREPARATION OF BACKGROUND AND OTHER COMPONENTS

From the black paper, cut three diamonds large enough to reach within 3″ of the top and the bottom of the matboard. Attach the diamonds to the left side of the matboard using double stick tape.

Spray paint the candlemold with black paint and, when it is dry, place it upside down in front of the right side of the matboard. Using floral clay, attach the pincup to what is now the top of the candlemold.

PROCEDURE

Place the largest helaconia flower on the back of the pincup, facing the front at an angle.

Place the second helaconia flower to the left facing in the opposite direction.

An extra piece of cut helaconia stem may be placed to the right if needed for balance.

Surround the base of the flowers with a circle of baby's breath with stems 3″ long. The baby's breath represents the clown's ruff.

Design 12

Class 4   IN THE MANNER OF MATISSE
*An interpretive design inspired by the works of
Henri Matisse. Background required.
Eligible for Creativity Award.*

SUPPLIES

Pedestal container with one
large and four small
openings

Pinholder, 3″ diameter

Floral clay

1 white matboard, 40″ by 32″

12 sheets of construction
paper, assorted colors

Rubber cement

1 medium round potato

4 tongue depressors or
popsicle sticks

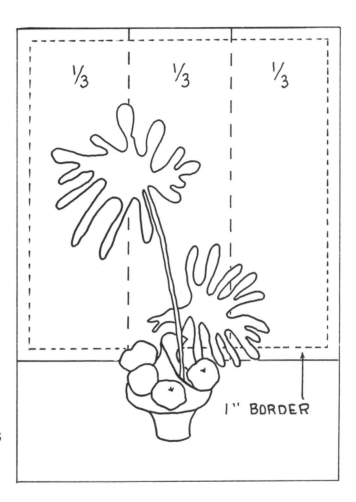

PLANT MATERIAL

2 monstera deliciosa leaves

5 apples

PREPARATION OF BACKGROUND

Using a pencil, lightly draw a 1″ margin completely around the
matboard. From the construction paper, cut out copies of shapes similar
to those of Matisse cut-outs. Apples and large leaves are typical of the
cut-out shapes found in the artist's work. Mentally divide the matboard
into three equal vertical sections, and attach the paper cut-outs with
rubber cement in the two outer sections of the matboard. The center is
left empty to emphasize the plant material.

PROCEDURE

Cut off the bottom one fourth of the potato and place cut side down on the left side of the pinholder, leaving some of the pin points free on the other side. To attach the potato to the pinholder, put the holder on the floor, then carefully place the potato on the desired section of the pinholder and press down hard on the potato with the heel of your foot.

Place the pinholder bearing the potato inside the container, making sure that the potato is touching the side of the container where the small holes are located. Secure the pinholder to the center of the container with floral clay.

Cut off, on a slant, the top of each of the four wooden sticks and insert the blunt ends through the small openings and into the potato. Impale an apple on each stick. Each apple should rest on the side of the container.

Place the two large leaves on the pinholder in the large center hole of the container facing in opposite directions and at different heights.

Rest the fifth apple in the large opening in the container to cover the potato and the pinholder.

VARIATION: Any large compote could be used for the container.

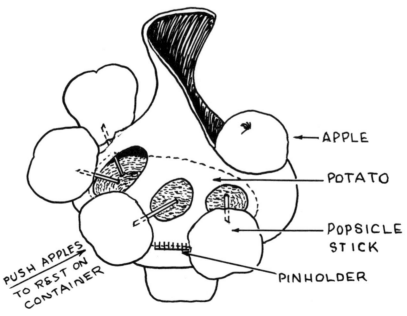

Design 13

Class 5 FIESTA TIME

An exhibition table expressing the spirit of Mexico. The exhibitor has complete freedom to choose the components. Some may be hung on the background. The designer may use fresh, dried and/or treated plant material. Accessories permitted.
Eligible for Creativity Award

SUPPLIES FROM MEXICO

1 silver candlestick used as a container

2 silver masks

1 silver plate

1 egg dish

1 amber goblet

1 pumpkin color matboard, 40" by 32"

½ pumpkin color matboard, 20" by 32"

Double stick tape

Floral clay

ADDITIONAL SUPPLIES

1 colorful napkin

1 bamboo plate holder

1 pincup, 2" diameter

Nylon filament (fishline)

PLANT MATERIAL

2 strelitzia flowers

2 citrus trifoliata branches

PREPARATION OF BACKGROUND

Place the large matboard upright for the background and the smaller piece in front as an underlay. Hang the silver masks from the top of the matboard by tying a length of nylon filament to each mask and securing the line to the back of the matboard with tape. The mask on the left should hang below the one on the right.

PREPARATION OF OTHER COMPONENTS

Turn the candlestick upside down so it will hold the pincup and place it on the right side of the background.

Tape the egg dish to the silver plate with double stick tape and stand them upright in the bamboo plate holder, which is placed on the left side. The goblet and napkin are placed in the center in front of the candlestick and plate.

DESIGN PROCEDURE

Place a tall branch of citrus trifoliata to the right, facing slightly toward the center. Trim off a few of the smaller branches to make more interesting spaces on the main branch.

Place a short piece of citrus trifoliata low in the front extending below the edge of the candlestick.

Place the larger strelitzia flower in the center back of the pincup facing toward the right. The smaller and shorter strelitzia is placed to the left, facing in the opposite direction.

NOTE: The eye of the viewer should be able to follow a continuous path from one component to the next throughout the exhibition table.

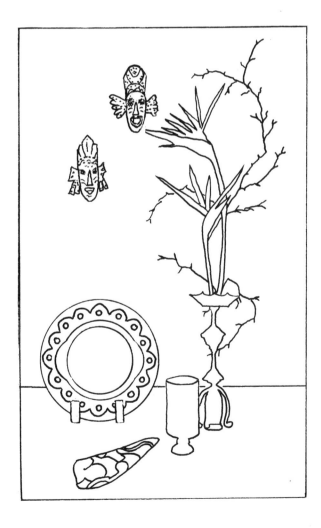

Section IV

Designs For Holidays

The new creative designs can be used in the home for holidays. Seasonal flowers such as calla lilies can be beautifully displayed in a creative line design for an Easter dinner table. In the summertime one thinks of the seashore, and what better time to try a transparency design, with flowers seen through the filigree of sea fans. It is exciting to think of other materials through which flowers can be seen. The very large leaves of the philodendron 'Monstera deliciosa' also offer exciting possibilities for a transparency design, as do dried palm leaves.

An eclectic design is one which combines the forms of more than one style and blends them together to create a new form. Combining two different design styles into a new concept is both challenging and rewarding.

Thanksgiving and Christmas are holidays that many wish to celebrate by decorating their homes both indoors and out. Fruits, flowers, evergreens, and man-made objects are used to create the holiday spirit. Hostesses entertaining families and friends have fun changing the colors of their table settings for the different occasions during the holiday season. For example, Christmas Eve might bring forth a gold and red color scheme with brass candlesticks holding cranberry-red candles, a lace cloth with a red liner underneath, red napkins, and cranberry-colored crystal. Christmas could be celebrated with silver and red—a white Madeira cut-work tablecloth and napkins, silver candlesticks with red candles and clear crystal. Then, on New Year's Eve, a silver and white color scheme with green crystal. Everyone enjoys the changes and it makes the holidays very special.

Kissing balls are perfect for hanging from indoor light fixtures or to use out of doors on the mailbox. The potato in the center supplies the moisture for the evergreens.

New Year's Day can be the occasion for using a fresh pear tree.

Most important of all, these designs can be made ahead of time and are long-lasting.

Design 14

Spring

An Eclectic Design

An eclectic design is a design created by borrowing from differing styles or periods and combining these features into a new concept. There may be more than one point of emergence, more than one center of interest, and some abstraction.

SUPPLIES

Large container with several
   openings
Large pinholder
Wire

PLANT MATERIAL

6 yellow gladioli
4 flowering forsythia branches
4 bare forsythia branches

PREPARATION

Attach the pinholder to the container.

Make 4 loops of varying sizes, using flowering forsythia branches.

Make 4 loops of varying sizes, using bare branches.

To make loops, see page 12.

PROCEDURE

A vertical design is placed in the opening on the left side of the container.

Cut flower #1 as tall as possible and place it in the center of the container.

Cut #2 shorter than #1 and place it to the left front of #1.

Cut #3 shorter than #2 and place it to the right front of #1.

Cut #4 shorter than #3 and place it in front of #1.

Cut #5 shorter than #4 and place it to the left of #4.

Cut #6 shorter than #5 and place it in front between #4 and #5.

A creative mass design is placed to the right of the vertical design.

The bare branch loops are numbered from #7 to #10 with #7 the largest and decreasing in size to the smallest, #10.

Place #7, the largest, next to flower #1.

Place #8 to the right and in front of #7.

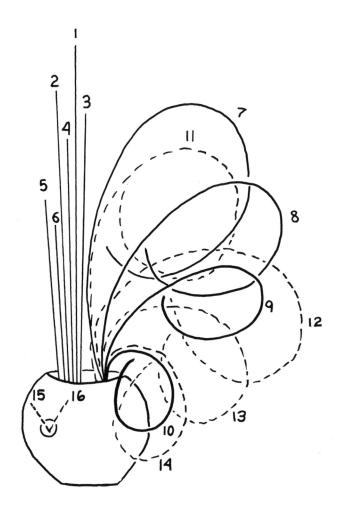

GLADS 1, 2, 3, 4, 5, 6   FLOWERING LOOPS _ _ _ _
BARE LOOPS 7, 8, 9, 10   11, 12, 13, 14

6" FLOWERING BRANCHES _ _ _ _
15 , 16

Place #9 to the right and in front of #8.

Place #10 in front of #9 leaning to the front.

The flowering loops, #11 through #14, are placed between the bare branch loops, starting with the largest in the back and coming forward. Two 6" pieces cut from the flowering branches, #15 and #16, are placed in the opening in the left front of the container.

Design 15

Easter   A Creative Line Design

Creative line designs use a minimum of plant material and sometimes emphasize the beauty of individual blooms or foliage. Man-made or found objects may provide the line material.

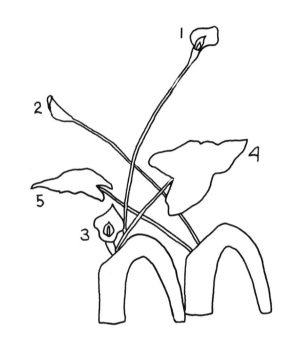

SUPPLIES

2 similar containers

Floral foam

PLANT MATERIAL

3 calla lilies

2 calla lily leaves

PREPARATION

Cut floral foam so it will fill half of each container and then fill the containers with water.

PROCEDURE

Cut flower #1 as long as possible and bend the stem slightly. See page 12. Place it in the container on the left so the tip of the flower is slightly over the top of the container on the right.

Cut flower #2 slightly shorter than #1 and place in the container on the right so the two flower stems cross about midway.

Cut flower #3 very short so the flower head is just above the opening in the left container.

Cut #4, large calla lily leaf, long enough so it fills the area above the right container. Place in the left container.

Cut #5 leaf long enough so it fills the area between #2 flower and #3 flower. Place in the right container.

VARIATION: This design may also be done: 1) in one long, narrow container with two pinholders; 2) in two similar containers placed horizontally to each other and touching for several inches at one end; or, 3) in two like containers placed at an angle, one on top of the other.

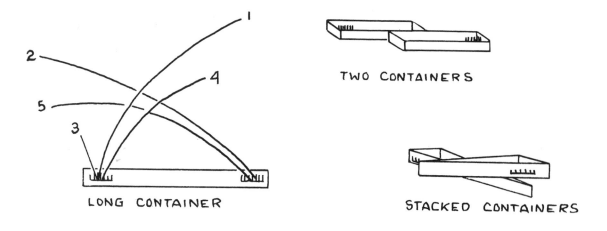

Design 16

Fourth Of July   A Transparency Design

A transparency is a creative design in which some components are seen through other components, increasing the three-dimensional effect.

PLANT MATERIAL

3 sprays of orange lilies

SUPPLIES

Creative container, 17″ by 3½″

Large pinholder

2 sea fans

1 balsa wood strip, ¼″ by ¼″ by 36″

Wire

PREPARATION

The edges of the sea fans may be trimmed with scissors to give a neater look. Cut out an uneven section from one of the fans. This cut-out becomes the third fan.

Sea fans need support in order to stand upright on a pinholder. Cut the balsa wood strip into six equal pieces. Wire two pieces of wood to each sea fan to form a stem. To do this, place each fan between two pieces of wood and run a wire through the fan and around the two pieces of wood several times. Before placing a fan on the pinholder, it may be necessary to re-cut the ends of the wood according to the depth of the container.

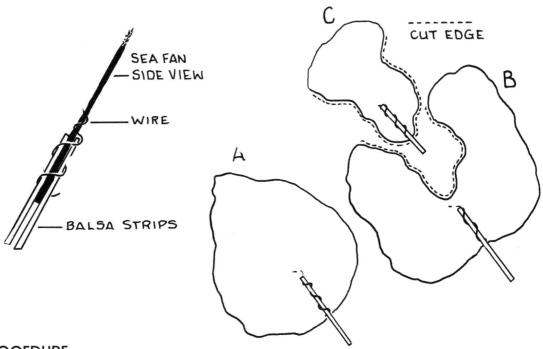

PROCEDURE

Place the three fans at different angles but touching each other on the right side.

Place fan A in the back.

Place fan B, the fan with the piece removed, in front of A.

Place fan C, the small cut-out, in front of B.

Cut #1 flower spray so flowers will show in the cut-out opening between fan A and B. Place on pinholder between A and B.

Cut #2 flower spray so it will extend slightly beyond the fans and place it low on the left side between fans A and B.

Cut the third flower spray in two pieces. Place #3 on the left between fans B and C, and #4 on the right in front of fan C.

Design 17

Thanksgiving   Pear Tree

SUPPLIES

Silver compote in lotus leaf
   pattern from India
12″ styrofoam cone
Pinholder, 2″ diameter
Round wooden toothpicks
Floral clay

PLANT MATERIAL

36 seckel pears
Boxwood sprigs

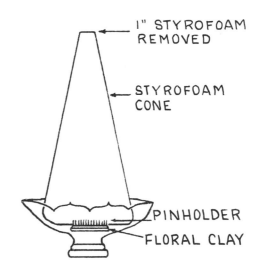

1″ STYROFOAM REMOVED

STYROFOAM CONE

PINHOLDER

FLORAL CLAY

PREPARATION

Cut off the top inch of the styrofoam cone and press the cone all the way down on the pinholder. This adds weight to the cone. Secure the cone to the compote by attaching floral clay to the outer edge of the cone.

PROCEDURE

Make a circle of pears around the bottom of the cone with all the pears leaning in the same direction. Remove a pear and place a toothpick in the cone at the height of the center of the pear. Impale the pear, at an angle, on the toothpick. Continue the circle of pears in the same way all around the bottom of the cone.

Working from the bottom to the top, add a second row of pears in the same manner, placing each pear in the new row of pears in between pears of the row below. Continue in this way until the cone is covered with pears. Place two toothpicks in the center top of the cone. Impale the prettiest pear upright on top of the cone.

Break the boxwood into small pieces and insert the sprigs in

between the pears, using slightly larger pieces around the bottom of the cone. On the top, use three or four small pieces of boxwood to fill out the tree effect.

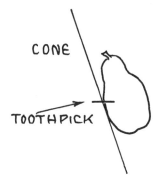

CONE

TOOTHPICK

PEARS SHOULD TOUCH
AND ALL FACE SAME
WAY WITH EXCEPTION
OF TOP PEAR.

Design 18

Christmas Eve   A Cranberry Topiary Tree

SUPPLIES

   18″ wooden dowel

   3″ flower pot

   Plaster of Paris

   Pebbles

   2 egg whites

   Sugar

   Pastry brush

   1 yard ¼″ red tube ribbon

   Wire

   Round wooden toothpicks

   Plastic wrap

PLANT MATERIAL

   1 large orange

   1 lb. cranberries

   4 holly sprigs

PREPARATION

   Paint the flower pot and wooden dowel dark green. Sharpen one end of the dowel in a pencil sharpener. To add weight, fill the flower pot half full of pebbles. This keeps the design from being top heavy.

   Mix plaster of Paris according to the directions on the box. Hold the dowel, point up, in the center of the flower pot, resting on the bottom. Pour in the plaster and hold the dowel upright until the plaster is set. When the plaster is completely dry, paint the exposed surface green.

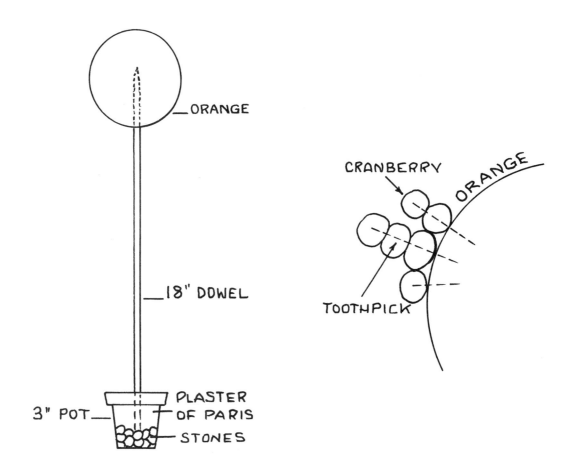

PROCEDURE

Cover the top of the pot with plastic wrap to keep it clean. Impale the orange, halfway, onto the pointed end of the dowel. Mix together the two egg whites and teaspoon of water.

Thread either one, two, or three cranberries on many toothpicks. Insert the toothpicks into the orange at random. Cover the orange completely, but allow a little of the orange color to show through.

Holding the dowel, position the cranberry-studded orange over the bowl of egg white mixture. Use a pastry brush to paint the mixture on the cranberries and orange. Immediately spoon on the granulated sugar until the fruit is well covered.

When the mixture of sugar and egg white is completely dry, add a red tube ribbon bow underneath the orange. Then wire the holly sprigs to the dowel at the top of the flower pot.

Design 19

Christmas   Kissing Ball

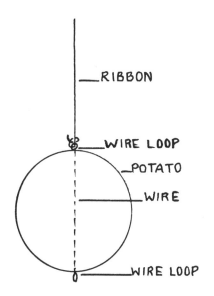

SUPPLIES

1 large round potato

12″ length of straight florist wire

2 yds. red ribbon, 1″ wide

2 floral picks

PLANT MATERIAL

1 lb. boxwood

PREPARATION

Wash the boxwood and cut into pieces approximately 3½″ long. Make the cuts on a slant to create pointed ends so it will be easier to push the boxwood into the potato.

Make a ribbon bow and attach it to a floral pick. Make streamers and attach them to another floral pick.

Insert a piece of wire, twice the length of the potato, through the potato. Make a loop of wire at the top of the potato so a ribbon can be attached to hang the kissing ball. Make another loop at the bottom to keep the potato from slipping off the wire.

PROCEDURE

Hold the potato upright and begin inserting the boxwood sprigs. Start by making two complete circles around the potato with the sprigs, one from top to bottom and one from side to side, dividing the potato into quarters. Fill in each section.

61

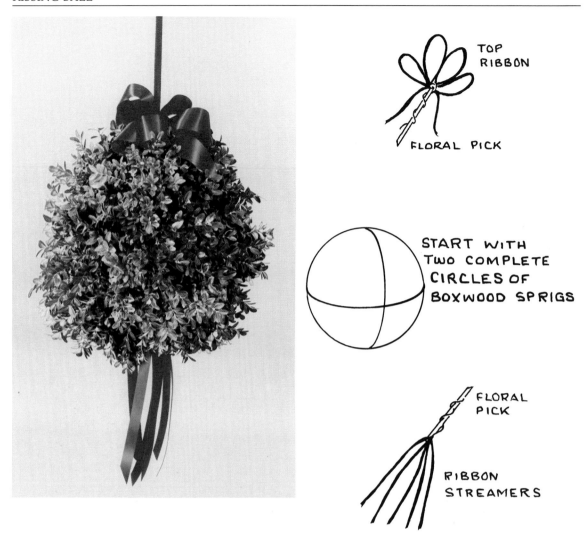

TOP RIBBON

FLORAL PICK

START WITH TWO COMPLETE CIRCLES OF BOXWOOD SPRIGS

FLORAL PICK

RIBBON STREAMERS

NOTE: Use an ice pick to make small holes in the potato, if there is difficulty inserting the boxwood.

For hanging, attach a ribbon to the wire loop on the top of the potato. Insert the red bow into the top of the boxwood. Then insert the streamers into the bottom of the boxwood.

Design 20

Christmas   Gesso Wreath

SUPPLIES

Gesso paint from art supply store

16″ styrofoam wreath

Styrofoam sheet, 2″ thick

Wooden floral picks, small size

3 bows of ½″ blue velvet ribbon

6 pewter candlesticks of various
   sizes

6 blue candles of various shades

An interesting assortment of dried
   plant material—nuts, pinecones,
   pods, dried flowers, holly, etc.
   Plastic material may be
   substituted for natural plant
   material.

PREPARATION

Attach each piece of dried or artificial plant material to a floral pick. Paint each one with white Gesso paint and insert in the styrofoam sheet to dry. Paint with a second coat if necessary to cover the color of the plant material.

When dry, insert the painted material into the wreath. Arrange it in an orderly manner, mixing the different shapes and forms. Attach the three blue velvet bows in the wreath equidistant from each other.

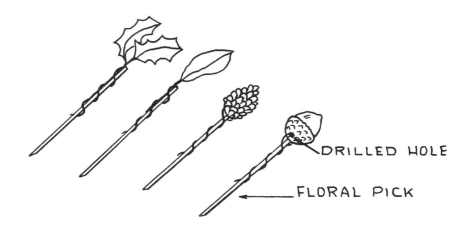

DRILLED HOLE

FLORAL PICK

TABLE SETTING SUGGESTION

Place the wreath in the middle of a round table set with a Wedgwood blue tablecloth and napkins and blue and white embossed Wedgwood china, and fill the center of the wreath with a collection of six different pewter candlesticks of various heights holding candles of different shades of blue.

VARIATION: If the color of the bows is changed to red, brass candlesticks with red candles could be placed on a white tablecloth.

Section V

Designs For The Table

A table setting is similar to the icing on a cake. It is the first thing seen when entering a dining room. It should be eye-catching and colorful. Even the smallest details should be considered and coordinated—the color of the tablecloth, napkins, china, and crystal, the color of the dining room itself. Function determines whether a table setting is formal or informal and should also regulate the type and style of cloth, napkins, china, crystal, and flowers. Formal table settings require fine china and crystal, while informal settings require heavier stoneware or pottery-type china and heavier glass. Roses and lilies are formal flowers, zinnias and marigolds are informal.

Be innovative with candles for very special occasions.

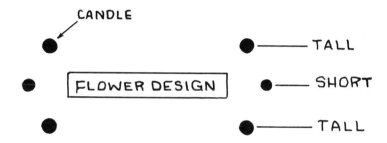

A. Four candles of the same height in tall candlesticks and two taller candles in shorter candlesticks.

B. Four candles placed at opposite corners of flower design.

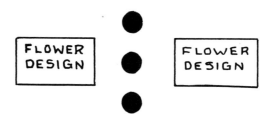

C. Two or three candles placed in the center of the table, between a pair of flower designs.

D. Two candles placed in the curves of low plant material, such as Scotch broom.

E. Six tall candles in candlesticks curving in opposite directons.

Design 21

Spring Luncheon   A Parallel Design

A parallel design has three or more vertical groupings of materials. Negative spaces between the groupings are important. Plant materials are positioned in a strong vertical manner. Units may be of one plant material, a combination of materials, or the same plant material repeated in each unit.

SUPPLIES

Long, narrow container, 17″ by 5″

3 small pinholders, 1½″ diameter

Floral clay

PLANT MATERIAL

8 purple liatris

7 purple tulips with white edges

PREPARATION

Using floral clay, attach pinholders to the container—one at each end and the third in the middle, but slightly closer to the left side.

PROCEDURE

These three groupings of flowers are considered one design, even though there is a definite separation between the groupings of flowers. The height and placement of each flower is dependent upon the height and placement of the flowers in the other groupings as well as the flowers in its own group.

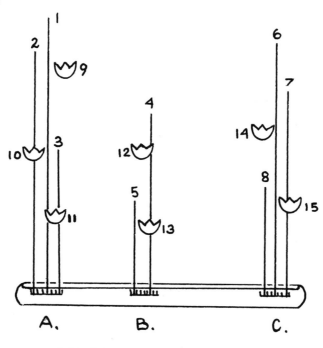

LIATRIS 1, 2, 3, 4, 5, 6, 7, 8
TULIPS 9, 10, 11, 12, 13, 14, 15

PINHOLDER A

Place the tallest liatris, #1, in the center back.

Cut liatris #2 shorter than #1 and place to the left front of #1.

Cut liatris #3 much shorter than #2 and place to the right front of #1.

PINHOLDER B

Cut liatris #4 slightly shorter than #2 and place in the center back.

Cut liatris #5 shorter than #3 and place to the left front of #4.

PINHOLDER C

Cut liatris #6 slightly shorter than #1 and place in the center back.

Cut liatris #7 shorter than #2 and place to the right front of #6.

Cut liatris #8 slighly shorter than #3 and place to the left front of #7.

PINHOLDER A

Cut tulip #9 shorter than #2 and place to the right front of #1.

Cut tulip #10 slighly shorter than #3 and place to the left front of #3.

Cut tulip #11 shorter than #5 and place between #10 and #3.

PINHOLDER B

Cut tulip #12 shorter than #3 and place to the left front of #4.

Cut tulip #13 shorter than #5 and place to the right front of #5.

PINHOLDER C

Cut tulip #14 slightly shorter than #4 and place to the left front of #6.

Cut tulip #15 slightly shorter than #8 and place to the right front of #8.

VARIATION: Five large zinnias could be used for this design. Zinnia foliage with its lovely opposite leaves completes the design without the use of any other plant material.

Design 22

Summer Patio Brunch

A Strawberry Tree

SUPPLIES

Small pedestal container or
  compote

10″ green styrofoam cone

Large pinholder, 3″ diameter

Floral clay

Round wooden toothpicks

Wire

PLANT MATERIAL

2 to 4 pints of strawberries, the
  larger the berries the fewer
  required

2 large bunches of parsley

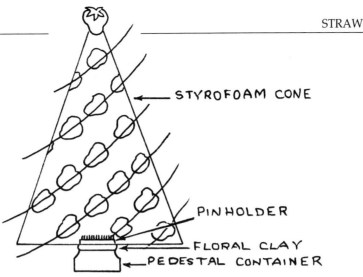

STYROFOAM CONE

PINHOLDER

FLORAL CLAY
PEDESTAL CONTAINER

PREPARATION

Attach the pinholder to the container with floral clay and then press the cone down onto the pinholder. Putting this design on a pedestal container raises the cone off the table and gives it the look of a tree.

Cut the wire into many 1″ pieces and bend each into a U-shape. These will be used to attach the parsley to the cone. Cut in half enough toothpicks to hold the strawberries.

PROCEDURE

Completely cover the cone with short pieces of parsley using the U-shaped pieces of wire.

To add strawberries, start at the top and work downward. Select the largest and most beautiful strawberry for the top. Insert a half toothpick in the top of the cone and then gently press the berry on to it. To avoid mashing the berries, the toothpicks should be inserted into the cone before impaling the berries.

Arrange a row of strawberries with pointed ends up, evenly spaced, around the top. In the next row down, arrange the strawberries so each piece of fruit is placed in the space between the berries in the row above. Continuing in this manner will produce a spiral pattern on the cone.

NOTE: A small bowl of powdered sugar placed on the table will encourage your guests to eat the berries.

VARIATION: Shrimp or cheese cubes.

Design 23

Thankgiving Dinner   Frosted Fruit

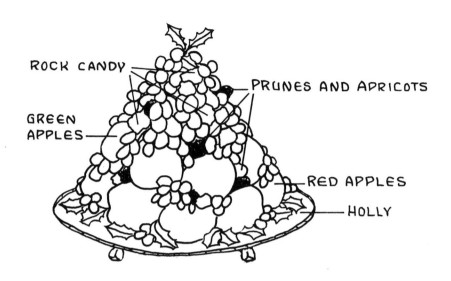

ROCK CANDY

PRUNES AND APRICOTS

GREEN APPLES

RED APPLES

HOLLY

SUPPLIES

Silver tray or meat platter

1½ cups coarse sugar crystals

10 pieces of rock candy

½ cup granulated sugar

3 egg whites

13 3″ wooden floral picks

Round wooden toothpicks

Pastry brush

Cake racks and cookie sheets

Aluminum foil

PLANT MATERIAL

7 very large red apples with stems

7 very large green apples with stems

2 lbs. red grapes

2 lbs. green grapes

12 dried prunes

12 dried apricots

8 3″ sprigs of holly

PREPARATION

Prepare the fruit the day before the design is to be used. Place several cake racks on cookie sheets. Slightly beat the whites of the three eggs and set aside. Mix ½ cup of granulated sugar with 1½ cups of coarse sugar in a small bowl.

Holding an apple by its stem, apply a light coat of egg white with a pastry brush. Then hold the apple over the bowl of sugar and spoon on the sugar until the apple is completely covered. Place on a cake rack to dry. Repeat for each apple.

Lightly brush grapes with egg white and lightly spoon on the sugar, shaking gently. Place on racks to dry.

Insert a toothpick in the end of each prune and apricot, then treat with egg white and sugar in the same way as the apples and grapes.

For holly sprigs, apply the egg white and sugar to the top side only.

Let the sugared material remain in a cool, dry place until ready to assemble.

PROCEDURE

Next day, when ready to assemble the fruit, cover the top of the silver tray with foil to protect it. Remove the wires from the floral picks.

Place the largest red apple, stem up, in the center of the tray and make a circle around it with the other six red apples. Remove one apple at a time from the circle and in that place insert a floral pick into the side of the center apple. Gently, but firmly, impale the apple on the pick in the center apple, making certain that the pick does not show. Continue in this manner until all six apples are attached to the center apple.

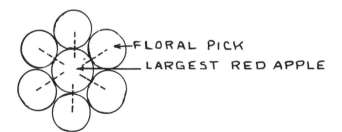

Insert a floral pick, upright, into the top of the center red apple and impale the largest green apple on it. Around it, arrange a ring of green apples so that each green apple rests between the two red apples below it. Then proceed to attach the second row of apples to the center apple in the same manner as the first row.

Begin layering the grapes on top of the apples, alternating the

colors of the grapes. Use toothpicks for support, if necessary. Make each layer of grapes slightly smaller than the one before, to create a mounded shape. Place the remaining small grape clusters in the spaces between the apples. Attach the prunes and apricots where color is needed or there is space between the fruit.

Place a large piece of rock candy on the top and the remainder throughout the fruit, using toothpicks for support, if necessary.

Trim off any foil that shows. Place the holly sprigs around the bottom of the fruit.

NOTE: Coarse crystal sugar is available from:

Pakrikas-Weiss Importers

1546 Second Avenue

New York, NY 10028

Design 24

New Year's Eve   A Creative Design

SUPPLIES

Silver bread basket

7 silver Christmas tree balls

Pincup, 3½" diameter

Silver tape

Silver spray paint

Flat white spray paint

Straight pins

PLANT MATERIAL

16 cattails

4 aspidistra leaves

PREPARATION

Weeks in advance, cut aspidistra leaves and roll their tips, securing with a straight pin. Allow them to dry while sitting in a container of water. This will take longer than letting them dry out of water, but the leaves will have a better shape. When they are completely dry, spray them with silver paint. Spray the dried cattails with a coat of flat white paint; and when this is dry, spray with a coat of silver.

Wrap the outside of the pincup with silver tape.

Line up all of the cattails on a table, arranging them in descending order of height with their stem ends extending beyond the table edge. Starting with the tallest on the left, work toward the shortest on the right.

Cut the first six according to
   diagram A.
#1 is 28" long and #6 is 18" long.

Cut the next five according to
   diagram B.
#7 is 19" long and #11 is 14" long.

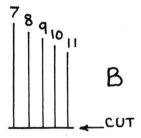

Cut the remaining 5 according to
   diagram C.
#12 is 18" and #16 is 12"

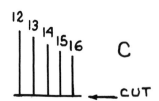

PROCEDURE

Turn the silver basket upside down with the Christmas balls underneath. Place the pincup in the top of the inverted base.

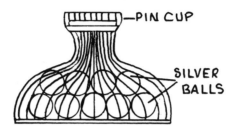

PLACEMENT IN PINCUP

Fan the three groups of cattails by placing each stem upright and ¼″ apart. Then slant each cattail in the direction indicated in diagram.

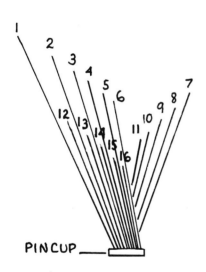

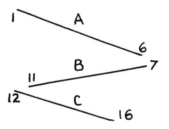

PINCUP GROUP PLACEMENT

A — 1, 2, 3, 4, 5, 6

B — 7, 8, 9, 10, 11

C — 12, 13, 14, 15, 16

Place the four aspidistra leaves around the cattail stems. Begin by placing the largest leaf next to the largest cattail.

Glossary

ABSTRACT DESIGN—A creative art form in which plant material and other components are used solely as line, form, color, and texture, with space, to create new images.

ACCESSORY—Something added which must be subordinate in the design. Anything in an arrangement in addition to plant material, container, base, background, or mechanics.

BACKGROUND—The surface against which an arrangement is seen.

BALANCE—Visual stability.

COMPONENTS—Physical material of which a design is composed: plant material, container, background, and mechanics.

CONTAINER—Any receptacle for plant material.

CREATIVE DESIGN—A design that results from the creative idea of the artist, using plant material and other components to organize the design elements within the limits of the principles of design.

CREATIVE LINE DESIGN—Uses a minimum of plant material/s and sometimes emphasizes the beauty of individual bloom/s or foliage. Man-made or found objects may provide the line material.

CREATIVE MASS DESIGN—A stylized mass design using more plant material than other present-day designs. There may be enclosed spaces, resulting from the placement of line materials, with these spaces being considered part of the mass. Groupings of plant materials of like colors, textures, and/or forms are massed along lines or spaces made by lines.

CREATIVITY—Characterized in flower design by originality in the choice of components or in the organization of the design elements within the limitation of the principles of design.

CREATIVITY AWARD—In a flower show governed by the rules of the National Council of State Garden Clubs, may be awarded to a blue ribbon winner scoring 95 points or more. The exhibitor has complete freedom to choose the components. The designer may use fresh, dried and/or treated plant material.

DESIGN ATTRIBUTES—Beauty, harmony, distinction, and expression.

DESIGN ELEMENTS—The basic visual qualities of a design—light, space, line, form, size, color, texture, and pattern.

DESIGN PRINCIPLES—Basic standards of art used to organize design elements—balance, proportion, scale, rhythm, dominance, and contrast.

ECLECTIC DESIGN—A creative design produced by borrowing from different styles or periods and combining these features into a new concept. There may be more than one point of emergence, more than one center of interest, and some abstraction.

EPERGNE—An ornamental centerpiece for table decoration consisting of several grouped dishes.

EXHIBITION TABLE—One in which design is not related to function.

FEATURE—A dominant object in a design.

FILLER PLANT MATERIAL—Transitional plant material used to fill in space between different plant forms.

GRADATION—A sequence in which there is regular and orderly change in size, form, color, or texture.

GROOMING—Cleaning flowers or plants by removing soil, spray residue, insect remains or damage, dead florets, leaves, etc.

HARDENING—Placing plant material in water several hours before arranging.

HORIZONTAL DESIGN—A design that is wider than it is tall.

LINE DESIGN—A design in which the linear pattern is dominant.

MASS DESIGN—Characterized by the use of a large quantity of plant material. The plant material is not crowded, but the design has a closed silhouette, meaning there are no open spaces within the outline of the design.

MATBOARD—A rigid board with a matte finish used for backgrounds.

MATKNIFE—A knife that is designed to cut matboard.

MECHANICS—Contrivances used to hold and control plant materials in designs.

ORIENTAL DESIGN—A design characterized by restraint in the quantity of plant material used, and having an open silhouette.

PARALLEL DESIGN—Has three or more vertical groupings of materials. Negative, or empty, spaces between the groupings are important.

PINCUP—Lead cup with needles to hold water and plant material.

PINHOLDER—Needles on a lead base to hold plant material.

SPIKE FLOWER—A lengthened flower cluster in which flowers are practically stemless. Examples: gladiolus, snapdragon, liatris.

TRANSPARENCY DESIGN—A creative design in which some components are seen through other components increasing the three dimensional effect.

UNDERLAY—That which is placed underneath (not a base). May be fabric or paper, and is usually a continuation of the material of the background; however, it may be of contrasting color or design.

VERTICAL DESIGN—Is one with a strong upward thrust and with greater height than width.

With appreciation to the National Council of State Garden Clubs, Inc. for permission to use selected definitions from its *HANDBOOK FOR FLOWER SHOWS.*

Index